Coal

Coal is one of the most valuable natural resources in the world. People have used it as a fuel for at least 3,000 years. The Industrial Revolution, which began in the mid-1700s, developed quickly because people discovered how to use coal as a fuel to smelt iron and drive steam engines to power the new machinery that was changing industry. More recently it has become a valuable source of chemicals from which a wide variety of substances, from medicines to plastics, can be made. Although it is now rivalled by oil, natural gas and nuclear power, coal seems likely to play a major part in our world for hundreds of years yet. Theodore Rowland-Entwistle is a former journalist who has written more than 30 reference books for readers of all ages. He is a Fellow of the Royal Geographical Society and the Zoological Society of London, and he holds an honours degree in history and geology.

Focus on
COAL

Theodore Rowland-Entwistle

Focus on Resources series

Alternative Energy	Paper
Coal	Plastics
Coffee	Rice
Cotton	Rubber
Dairy Produce	Seafood
Fruit	Silver
Gas	Soya
Gold	Sugar
Grain	Tea
Iron and Steel	Timber
Nuclear Fuel	Water
Oil	Wool

Cover *A bucket-wheel dredge at work in an Australian opencast mine.*
Frontispiece *A coal-cutting shearer in action.*

First published in 1987 by
Wayland (Publishers) Ltd
61 Western Road, Hove
East Sussex BN3 1JD, England

© Copyright 1987 Wayland (Publishers) Ltd
Phototypeset by Kalligraphics Ltd, Redhill, Surrey
Printed in Italy by G. Canale & C.S.p.A., Turin
Bound in Britain at The Bath Press, Avon

British Library Cataloguing in Publication Data

Rowland-Entwistle, Theodore
    Focus on coal. — (Focus on resources
    series)
    1. Coal — Juvenile literature
    I. Title
    553.2′4   TN801

ISBN 0–85078–969–9

12.95

Contents

1. What is coal?

Coal is a soft black or brown rock and one of our most valuable natural resources. We burn it to produce heat and energy. It is often known as a fossil fuel, because it is the fossilized remains of plants that grew millions of years ago. Coal is also an important source of chemicals, from which such things as dyes and synthetic rubber can be made.

Coal consists largely of the chemical element carbon, which gives it its black colour. It also contains the gases hydrogen, nitrogen and oxygen, all of which burn readily. Some of these chemicals are in the form of hydrocarbons,

A huge rotary excavator at an opencast pit at Bogytr in the USSR.

compounds of hydrogen and carbon, which are also found in petroleum and natural gas.

Although coal occurs in most parts of the world, it is very unevenly distributed. The largest reserves of coal are in North America, Europe and northern Asia. There are enough known coal deposits to last for the next three or four hundred years, and it is not known how much coal is yet to be discovered.

Coal is formed in layers, known as seams. Some are only a few millimetres thick, but most seams are about one or two m (3–6 ft) thick. A few can be 30 m (100 ft) thick. The seams, which lie at different depths, are sandwiched between layers of other rocks. Seams near the surface can be reached easily, while others lie far underground, at depths up to 3 km (1.9 miles), and miners must sink deep shafts to reach them.

Many people heat their homes by burning coal on open fires.

Merry-go-round trains provide power stations with a constant supply of coal straight from the mine.

7

2. How coal was formed

Many millions of years ago, huge forests grew on swampy land. The climate was warm and damp. The trees, unlike the forest trees you can see today, were giant ferns, as tall as our oak or pine trees. These forests survived for thousands of years. When the trees died they crashed to the ground and rotted there. In time the trees and their leaves formed a thick layer of partly rotted vegetable matter.

After many years rivers rose and washed over the forests, burying them under layers of sand and mud. This process happened many times, forming layers of vegetable matter sandwiched by layers of other material. Eventually the sea covered the sandwich, and more sand and mud were washed over to build up layers several thousand metres thick.

Over millions of years rotting vegetation was compressed to form layers of coal.

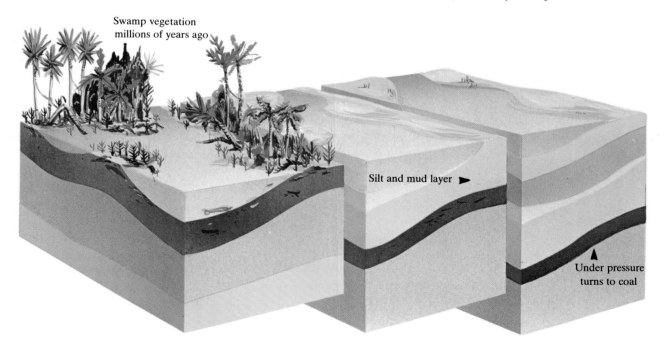

Swamp vegetation millions of years ago

Silt and mud layer ▶

Under pressure turns to coal

As the layers became more deeply buried they were compressed and heated up. The vegetable matter changed into the rock we know as coal, sands became sandstone and muds formed shales and mudstone.

Coal has been formed at various times in the Earth's long history, from the Devonian Period, beginning around 400 million years ago, to the present day. You can see the early stages of coal in swampland now, where it forms the semi-

Trees growing in swamps could one day rot down and eventually turn into coal.

rotted material we call peat.

The period between 280 and 345 million years ago is known as the Carboniferous Period, because so much coal, which is largely carbon, was formed then, especially in North America and Europe. Most of the coal in Australia was formed after the Carboniferous Period.

9

3. Seams and faults

When the coal measures were formed the various layers – known as strata – were more or less level. If they were still level now they would be comparatively easy to find and dig out. However, over millions of years the rocks of the Earth's surface have folded, tilted and broken, so the neat sandwich has been distorted. Most of these movements happen so slowly we cannot detect them, but occasionally we do see movement when earthquakes occur.

The simplest movement the miner meets with is tilting, when all the layers of rock have tipped over and lie at an angle. The slope is often very steep, and can even be vertical.

Often the layers are folded, just as if you took a pile of blankets and crumpled them together from each side. Strata may dip down to form a trough, known as a syncline, or they may arch upwards, forming an anticline.

A fault is a place where the strata have broken. Miners come across faults when they are digging out the coal. The coal seam suddenly comes to an end and the miners are confronted with a wall of different rock. The difference in level between the end of the seam and where it starts again is called the 'throw'. This may be less than a metre (3 ft), or several hundred times as great, and the throw may go either up or down.

Sometimes the coal seam may be interrupted by a layer of sandstone, deposited millions of years ago by a river which cut across the seam. This is known as a 'washout'.

This diagram shows the various geological features that can interrupt a coal seam.

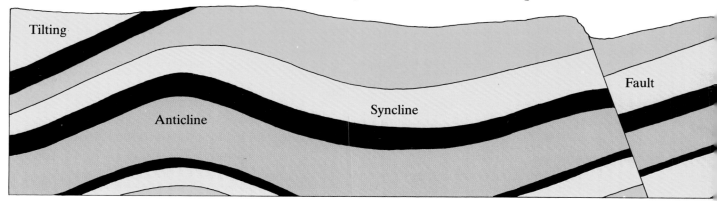

Tilting

Anticline

Syncline

Fault

Above *The faults show up clearly in this rock formation.*

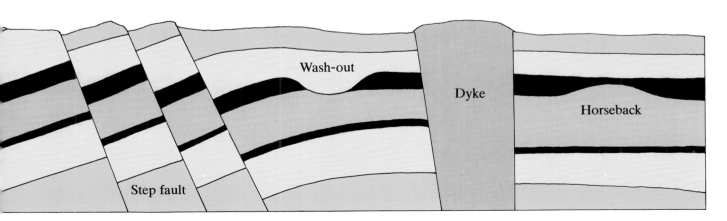

Step fault

Wash-out

Dyke

Horseback

4. Types of coal

The term 'ranks' is used to describe the various types of coal. The more carbon the coal contains the higher the rank.

Peat that is found on the surface is not coal, because it has not yet been buried and compressed to form rock. But all coal once passed through a peat stage. Peat is formed in boggy conditions. It is wet when it is dug out, but it can be dried and used as fuel. It is widely used in the Soviet Union and parts of Ireland as fuel.

The lowest rank of true coal is lignite, some of which is known as brown coal because of its colour. It is a comparatively young coal, which crumbles readily, and traces of the original plant material can still be seen in it. There are large deposits of lignite in Australia and North

All coal once passed through a peat stage. Here we see peat being dug up to use as fuel.

The various types of coal. Top, from left to right: Phurnacite, Anthracite, Sunbrite; bottom, left to right: Housecoal, Coalite, Homefire, Rexco.

America, where it is most usually burned in power stations.

Bituminous coal is the most common kind of coal, and there are many ranks of it. It is the fuel most often burned in household fireplaces and in factories. It consists of alternate layers of bright and dull material, and breaks readily into large rectangular blocks. Some bituminous coal, however, is dull and shows no layers. It is known as cannel coal, because it produces a long bright flame like a candle.

The hardest coal is anthracite, which burns with hardly any smoke. It is used for household fires and central heating furnaces. A freshly-broken piece of anthracite has a surface with an almost metallic shine.

5. Coal around the world

Although every continent has reserves of coal, the main coalfields lie in North America, Europe, northern Asia and Australia.

North America has about half the world's known coal reserves, and the USA is the largest producer of hard coal.

The Morwell opencast mine in Victoria, one of the largest in Australia.

A lot of the coal in South America lies deep under the rainforests and is hard to reach. Colombia, Brazil, Chile and Argentina are the only countries with good known coal reserves.

Europe has a band of rich coalfields stretching from Britain in the west, through France, Belgium, the Netherlands, West and East Germany, Poland and Czechoslovakia.

The Soviet Union, which lies partly in Europe

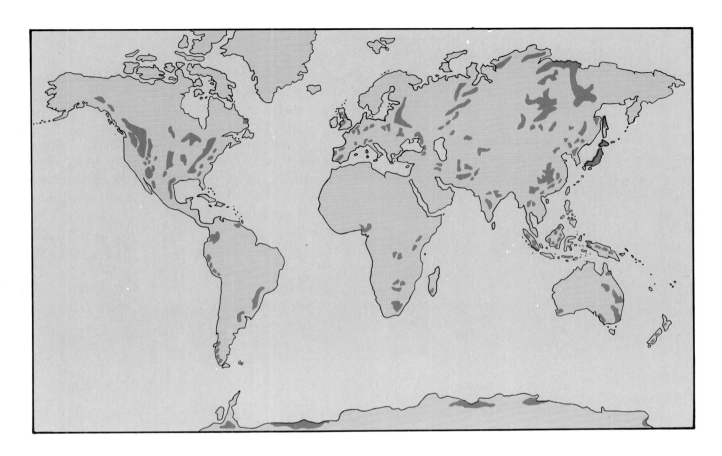

Map showing where the world's major known coal deposits are found.

and partly in Asia, has three great coalfields – in the Donets River basin in the Ukraine; at Kuznetsk near the River Volga; and around Karaganda in Kazakhstan.

Asia's biggest reserves lie in China, which is the world's second largest coal producer. Other leading producers are India, North and South Korea and Japan.

Africa's biggest coalfields are in South Africa and Zimbabwe. Only six of Africa's 48 other countries mine any coal – Algeria, Morocco, Mozambique, Nigeria, Tanzania and Zaïre.

Australia is the world's eighth largest producer of hard coal. It has a vast deposit of lignite in Victoria, nearly 240 m (780 ft) thick. New Zealand also produces coal.

Antarctica has deposits of coal, but since it is covered by 80 per cent of the world's ice, coal production would be difficult.

6. Looking for coal

Ancient histories tell us that the Chinese were using coal about 3,000 years ago. Like other early users, they probably found coal as an outcrop — that is, appearing above the surface of the ground. Such outcrops can be seen on river banks or on the sides of valleys and hills.

Having discovered coal in the sides of hills, miners would tunnel in to dig it out. They would also dig down from the top of the hill, knowing that the seam would probably continue underground, following a line from where it was last seen.

Geologists examine the results of a seismic survey.

Above *A coal sample extracted during exploratory drilling for coal.*

Modern coal exploration is the work of geologists: scientists who study rocks and the structure of the Earth. In the first stage, they study the known geology of an area to work out where coal might be. Then they carry out a seismic survey, by setting off small explosions to send shock waves down through the ground. Different rock layers, including coal, reflect the waves at different speeds. The reflections are picked up by geophones – microphones buried in the ground.

The signals picked up by the geophones are analyzed by computers, which produce accurate charts. These show the position of the coal seams, how much they slope and in which direction, and any faults in the rocks.

Once the seismic survey is complete the geologists drill boreholes to take samples of the rock deep underground. They lower electronic devices down the boreholes to measure such things as moisture, natural radioactivity and rock density. Drilling is also used to locate coal under the sea.

Below *Laying the charges that will send shock waves down through the ground.*

7. Mining methods

In opencast mining coal is found close to the surface. This mine is in Cologne, in West Germany.

There are two basic methods of mining coal. One is deep mining, which means digging down into the ground to find the coal seams. The other, used when coal lies near the surface, is called either opencast, open cut or strip mining. In this method the overlying soil is removed, and the coal is stripped away.

Both methods have disadvantages. In opencast mining a very large area of land must be worked, which causes obvious damage to the countryside. Deep mines take up less room, but waste materials brought to the surface have to be piled up in unsightly slag-heaps. In deep pits the miners must work far underground, in dark and often dangerous conditions.

There are two ways of reaching coal in deep mines. The first way involves sinking a shaft straight down to the level of the seams, and then driving horizontal tunnels off from this to extract the coal. The miners and their machinery must be lowered down the shaft in lifts, and the coal has to be hauled out the same way.

In a drift mine a tunnel known as an adit slopes down to the level of the coal seams. The miners and their equipment travel on a railway, while the coal is brought up the adit to the surface on a conveyor belt. Drift mines are dug when the coal seam starts close to the surface, or lies under a hill.

Above *The entrance to a drift mine, showing the conveyor belt that brings the coal up.*

Below *Deep mines take up less room than opencast mines, but unsightly waste materials are a problem.*

8. Starting a deep mine

Mines vary greatly in depth. For example, in the USA the average depth is 80 m (260 ft), while in Britain the average depth is 450 m (1,475 ft).

To sink a shaft, the miners drill about 100 small holes 2.4 m (8 ft) deep, fill them with explosives, and then fire them. This breaks up the

A twin-boom roadheading machine, which cuts the tunnels in a deep mine.

rock, which is then loaded into a giant bucket and hauled to the surface. As the hole grows deeper the walls are lined with concrete, up to 1.4 m (4½ ft) thick, to keep out water and prevent the sides from caving in. Huge drilling machines which will bore straight into the ground are now being developed. A mine needs at least two shafts, one for ventilation.

The roads, as the deep tunnels are known, are

cut with a huge machine called a roadheader. It has one or more rotating heads, each carrying hardened steel cutting picks, which bite into the rock. Other machines gather up the broken rock and load it on to conveyor belts or into trucks which carry it out of the mine. In very hard strata machines drill small holes, which are packed with explosives to blast out the rock.

To protect the miners there is a device called a walking canopy. It covers the space between the permanent tunnel supports and the working face, so that roof falls will not trap or injure the men. Laser beams are used to mark the centre of the working coalface and so keep the tunnel straight.

Sinking a shaft at one of the world's largest deep mines in Selby, Yorkshire.

9. Cutting the coal

There are two working systems in deep mines. The older method is called pillar and stall, or room and pillar. Sections of coal, the pillars, are left in place to support the roof. The part where the coal is removed is called the stall, or room. This method is still common in the USA.

In Europe and most other parts of the world – and increasingly in the USA – the longwall system is used. In this a huge coal-cutting machine works to and fro along the coalface, which may be as much as 300 m (330 yds) long. As the miners cut and remove the coal, they prop up the roof with hydraulic supports. When the coal-cutting machinery has advanced far enough the roof supports are moved forward and the roof is allowed to subside behind.

Only one man is needed to operate the elec-

This diagram shows the room and pillar and the longwall methods of mining.

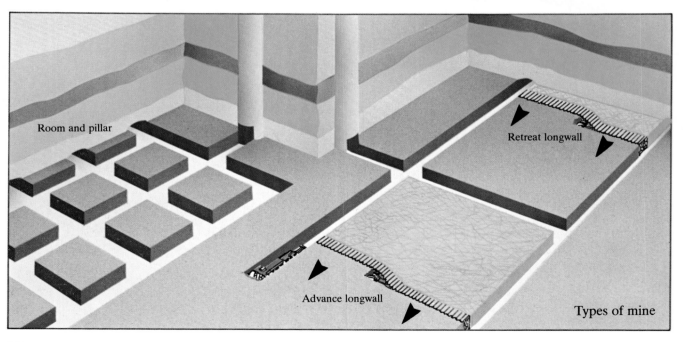

Room and pillar

Retreat longwall

Advance longwall

Types of mine

A coal-cutting shearer working along the coalface. The water sprays keep the dust down.

trically-driven power-loader, which cuts the coal to a depth of 1 m (3 ft) and loads it on to a conveyor belt. Water is sprayed on the coalface to keep the dust down. In the most modern mines an automatic steering system keeps the cutter within the coal seam.

In older mining methods the coal is shattered by small, controlled explosions in holes drilled in the face, or by releasing compressed air into the holes. Machines then scoop it up and load it into trucks or on to conveyor belts.

10. Opencast mining

Opencast mining is used extensively in the USA and Australia, and it is also used for some of the lignite (brown coal) deposits in Continental Europe. In Britain only 5 per cent of coal is mined in this way. Opencast techniques can be used to extract coal from seams up to 60 (200 ft) below ground level.

Because opencast working makes such a mess, care must be taken, especially in crowded countries such as Britain, to protect people living nearby. The overlying rock and soil are stripped off and piled around the edge of the site to form a screen. Work always stops at night and on Sundays.

Opencast mining in progress on derelict land near Ilkeston, Derbyshire.

Giant excavators remove the rock and soil, and then scoop out the coal. In areas near villages and towns these excavators are electrically powered to cut down noise. To give you some idea of their size, the largest excavator used in Britain, nicknamed 'Big Geordie', can remove 100 tonnes of material with one bite of its bucket, which can hold two large cars side by side.

Reversing these and other huge vehicles could be dangerous, so the driver has television cameras at the back of the vehicle to show him what lies behind him. Some vehicles have a radar system called ALBERT (Analogue Linear Bi-polar Electronic Ranging Transducer). It can distinguish people from other objects, and it automatically applies the brakes if anyone steps into the path of the reversing vehicle.

After the coal has been removed the rock and topsoil are put back and the site is restored to farmland or parkland.

Above *After the mining is completed, the opencast site is restored to parkland.*

The dragline excavator 'Big Geordie' at work on an opencast mining site.

25

11. Underground transport

Checking that the coal-carrying conveyor belt is running smoothly, in a drift mine in Yorkshire.

As more and more coal is extracted, so the coal-faces being worked move further away from the pit shaft. Transporting men to and from work and bringing the coal to the surface is therefore a major operation. In some pits the miners may have to travel as far as 11 km (7 miles) to get to the coalface.

Where tunnels are big enough trains pulled by electric or diesel engines are used. The electric trains pick up their current from overhead wires. For smaller side tunnels where overhead lines cannot be laid, battery-powered trains are coming into use.

Many coal seams, and therefore the mine

Above *Miners prepare to descend the shaft in the lift-car, or cage.*

used the coal is carried in cars pulled by diesel or electric engines.

At the foot of the main shaft the coal is loaded into giant skips and hauled to the surface. The miners travel in large lift-cars, known as cages. Computers and electronic sensors monitor the position of every skip and cage. At any suggestion of trouble they cut off the power and apply the brakes.

Below *High-speed trains that carry 300 men at a time to working districts 6 km out under the North Sea.*

tunnels, dip up and down, with slopes that are too steep for the trains. In such places the train is pulled along by a steel cable, driven by an electric motor at one end of the run, but radio-controlled by the train's guard.

Most of the coal is carried on conveyor belts, which may be several kilometres long. Electronic sensors are installed at intervals along the belt system to detect overheating or excessive wear. Where conveyor belts cannot be

12. Preparing the coal for sale

Coal taken straight from a deep or opencast mine is not ready for sale. Some of it is powder, some is in lumps too large to use, and it is also mixed up with rock and other debris. It must be cleaned and graded, and if necessary broken up. This process is carried out in a special preparation plant.

Most of the rock and other debris is denser and heavier than coal. To separate the two, the material from the mine is put into a bath of liquid that has a specific gravity greater than

Coal from opencast sites is not ready for sale, as it is mixed with rock and other debris.

coal, but less than the other rocks. A mixture of water and magnetite (a form of iron oxide) is often used. The coal floats and the other material sinks.

Coal dust can be separated from other materials by passing it through a frothy mixture of oil and water. The coal sticks to the oily froth while rock particles sink. The froth and coal are then skimmed off.

Machines sort the coal into sizes by passing it through screens like giant sieves. Other machines using devices such as X-rays sort the coal into different ranks, which determine what it can be used for.

Even coal dust can be used. Some power station furnaces burn it as it is, but for use in the home it can be made into blocks called briquettes, by mixing it with tar.

Below *The computerized control room of the coal preparation plant.*

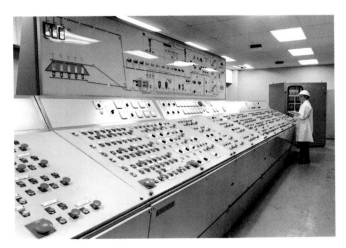

Below *Automated preparation plants clean and grade coal before it is sent to consumers.*

13. Transport from the pithead

Coal is carried from the pits by road, rail and water. In London in the 1500s the fuel was known as 'sea-cole' because it was brought to the city by ship from north-east England.

After processing, the coal is taken to automated loading centres. Overhead hoppers and bunkers hold thousands of tonnes of coal. Freight trains made up of permanently coupled wagons pass under the hoppers, which can load four wagons at a time. A train can be loaded and checked within an hour.

In most countries, power stations use the largest amounts of coal. Trains shuttle to and fro between the mines and the power station, carrying from 1,000 to 9,000 tonnes of coal. If the power stations are near the pithead the coal can be carried on conveyor belts. One conveyor belt in Arizona in the USA is 22 km (14 miles) long.

Pipelines from modern lorries deliver coal straight to industrial consumers' bunkers.

A train is loaded with coal as it passes beneath a rapid-loading bunker.

In many countries coal is delivered by road to factories and other industrial plants. Some lorries just tip their loads out, but increasingly they are being equipped with small conveyor belts or pipelines to deliver the coal directly into the customer's bunkers. The coal is forced along pipelines by compressed air.

In many countries coal is mixed with water to form a mixture called slurry. The slurry is pumped along giant pipelines over many kilometres. Where pits are near rivers or canals the coal is carried by barge.

Lorries carrying coal from an opencast mine in the USA.

14. Using coal

This coal mine supplies coal to the adjacent power station.

The most common way of using coal is to burn it to produce heat. This heat can be used directly, as in a coal fire, or to heat water to make steam, which can drive machines or electric generators.

Two other commonly-used fuels are made from coal: coke and gas. To make these, coal is heated in an airtight oven. Without the oxygen in air it cannot burn. The heat drives out coal-tar, light oils, ammonia and gas, leaving coke, which is hard and full of tiny holes. Coke is used in the manufacture of steel. Coal gas is used as a fuel when no natural gas is available.

Above *Coke is often used in the manufacture of steel.*

Almost anything that can be made from petroleum can be made from coal, including petrol and diesel oil. We use coal products every day without realizing it. Antiseptics for wounds, drugs to cure illnesses, dyes for cloth, detergents, perfumes and nail varnish are all made from coal.

Out in the garden, fertilizers that help plants to grow, weedkillers and insecticides can all be made from coal. We even eat it in the form of saccharin, the sugar substitute. Explosives, artificial fibres such as nylon, synthetic rubber, and plastics can all be made from coal.

Right *This power station has a jetty, (extreme right) which takes deliveries of coal.*

15. Early mining

The first people to use coal quarried it from hillsides and other outcrop sites. Later they dug for it, making a shaft down to the coal seam and then digging out a bell-shaped pit. Coal miners first began digging tunnels from the bottom of shafts about 600 years ago.

Early mining was a laborious business. The coal had to be dragged along underground tunnels on sledges, and hauled up the shaft with primitive cranes, or carried up ladders on people's backs. The first railways were built in the early 1500s to enable miners to haul coal up

Until very recently pit ponies were used underground to pull the coal wagons.

Miners loading coal into wagons in England in the 1920s.

sloping tunnels to the surface. Deep mining was impossible because of flooding, until the first steam-driven water pumps were invented around 1700.

Work in mines was hard, difficult and dangerous. Men lay on their backs in workings less than a metre high, cutting at the coal with picks. Children as young as five and women were employed underground, pulling laden trucks along low, narrow tunnels. During the 1800s most countries banned the employment of women and children underground.

Pit ponies were used to pull wagons underground until very recently. A few remain in use in some difficult mines in Britain, where they haul supplies up to new workings before machinery can be installed. It is planned to stop using pit ponies altogether.

Women and children used to work in mines, in dark and dangerous conditions.

35

16. The human cost

Coal mining is a dangerous job. Explosions, roof falls and fire are constant hazards. The worst pit disaster was in China in 1942, when an explosion at Honkeiko Pit killed 1,572 miners.

Even today, in spite of modern safety precautions, accidents still happen, but the death rate in the world's pits has been steadily falling. In 1950, 476 men were killed in Britain's mines, but only 22 deaths occurred in a similar period in 1983-84.

Not all mining disasters occur underground. One of the worst took place at Aberfan, in South Wales, on 21 October 1966. An old slag-heap 240 m (300 ft) high, slipped after heavy rain and engulfed a primary school at its foot. There were 144 deaths, most of them young children.

Miners carry victims from the shaft of a Japanese mine, after an underground explosion in 1963 killed 450 men and injured 900 more.

A rescue worker shows the equipment used when working underground after explosions.

The coal dust underground is a serious health hazard, and breathing it for many years can leave miners with a lung disease called pneumoconiosis. Today, water sprays are used to help keep down dust, and miners are encouraged to wear masks. Their lungs are checked regularly by X-ray so that any disease can be detected and treated quickly.

Opposite *In 1966 a slag-heap at Aberfan in Wales slipped and buried a primary school.*

17. Safety in the mines

A serious hazard in mines is explosive methane gas, which miners call firedamp. Miners need light to work by, and the use of candles and naked lights in the past led to many explosions. In 1815 the leading British scientist of the day, Sir Humphry Davy, invented the safety lamp, in which the flame was protected by a fine wire mesh. Nowadays, miners have an electric lamp fitted to their helmets, which runs off a battery.

Computer-controlled electronic devices are used today to detect the presence of firedamp. Ventilation systems, driven by huge fans, draw all dangerous gases up the ventilation shaft. About 20 tonnes of fresh air are circulated for every tonne of coal mined.

Below *A deputy inspects coalface operations at a mine in Yorkshire.*

Above *The powered supports of the tunnel help prevent the roof from collapsing.*

Rescue teams entering a mine after an explosion test constantly for poisonous carbon monoxide. Until the 1980s the only reliable way was to take a canary in a cage into the mine.

The canary reacted to carbon monoxide much faster than the men, so the rescuers could retreat or put on breathing apparatus. The canary was revived with a whiff of oxygen. Nowadays, an electronic device, which can detect methane and other gases, as well as carbon monoxide, is replacing the canaries.

Other safety measures include fire-detection systems, better pit props for the roof, regular inspection to detect rock movements, and educating miners in safety. Pumps work constantly to remove water. In some mines 33 tonnes of water are pumped out for every tonne of coal extracted.

A surveyor carries out a safety inspection. To the right is the conveyor belt that carries the coal.

18. Coal and the environment

An opencast site in Derbyshire, during mining operations.

Coal-mining areas used to be unsightly places. They were dominated by the pithead gear, the coal preparation plant and huge untidy spoil tips. In many countries the housing provided for miners and their families was cramped and badly built.

Today's mining villages are much brighter and cleaner than they used to be. With cars, miners can live further from the mine and drive to work. The pithead at a new mine is designed to blend in as far as possible with the landscape, and attempts are being made to improve old coal mines and their surroundings.

Slag-heaps are less of a problem then they used to be, because a great deal of the rock

brought up (one tonne for every two tonnes of coal) is sold as minestone for building roads. Better sorting ensures that very little coal is discarded as waste. Old tips are being levelled and landscaped, and used as farmland.

Damage to the environment can also be caused when old workings collapse underground, causing the surface land to subside. With new mines geologists carry out careful

The same site after restoration work has been carried out.

surveys before work begins and steps are taken to make sure that subsidence is controlled.

Harm is also caused to the countryside by the transportation of coal by road. Large numbers of heavy lorries, on narrow roads not designed for such traffic, produce noise and air pollution.

41

19. The future

The modern industrial world needs large quantities of fuel to provide energy. At present the main sources of energy are hydro-electric schemes, oil, natural gas, nuclear power – and, of course, coal.

Coal was the first of the three fossil fuels to be exploited, and it seems likely that it will still be available when supplies of the other two, oil and natural gas, are exhausted. The use of nuclear power has grown dramatically, but as the Chernobyl disaster in the Ukraine in 1986 showed, it can threaten widespread damage to health and the environment, possibly over a long period, if an accident happens. Hydro-electric schemes are available only in countries with suitable rivers.

The future of the coal industry seems bright provided the coal can be extracted cheaply and efficiently. The mine of the future will probably employ fewer men underground, with much of the work being done by machines controlled from the surface by computers.

An idea now being tested in the USA is to burn the coal underground to make it release gas, which can then be piped to the surface. The fire is kept alight by injecting oxygen to the seam.

Since it is likely that supplies of coal will outlast oil, research is being carried out into the use of coal to make products normally made

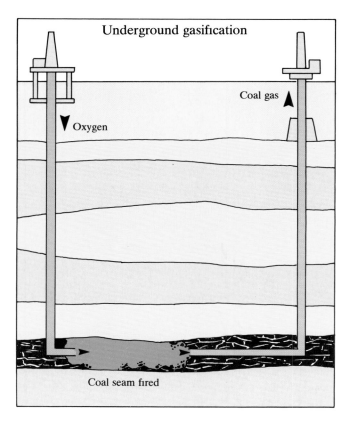

An idea now being tested is to burn coal underground to make it release gas.

from oil. It is possible that by the beginning of the next century both cars and aircraft will be powered by fuel made from coal.

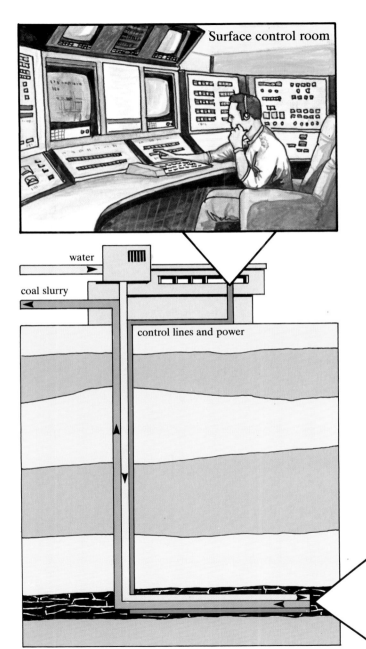

Surface control room

water

coal slurry

control lines and power

Oil found in the sea will probably be exhausted long before coal supplies run out.

Left *The mine of the future may be fully-automated, needing no underground workers.*

Automated continuous miner

Facts and figures

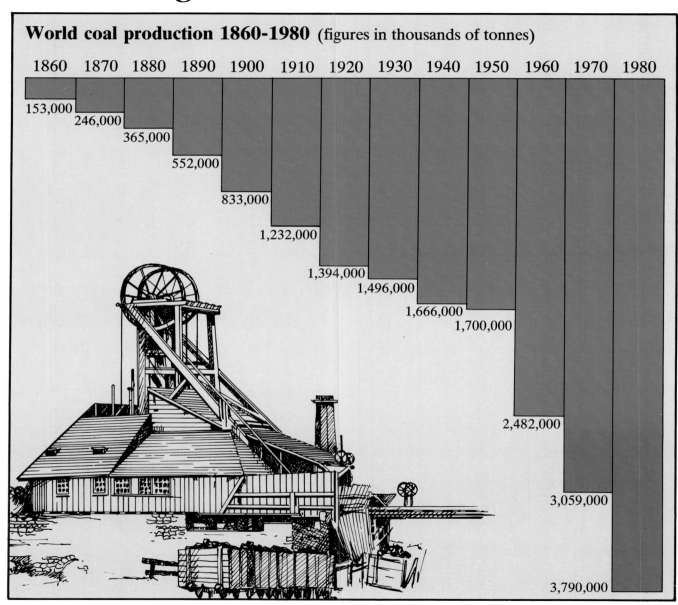

World coal production 1860-1980 (figures in thousands of tonnes)

| 1860 | 1870 | 1880 | 1890 | 1900 | 1910 | 1920 | 1930 | 1940 | 1950 | 1960 | 1970 | 1980 |

153,000

246,000

365,000

552,000

833,000

1,232,000

1,394,000

1,496,000

1,666,000

1,700,000

2,482,000

3,059,000

3,790,000

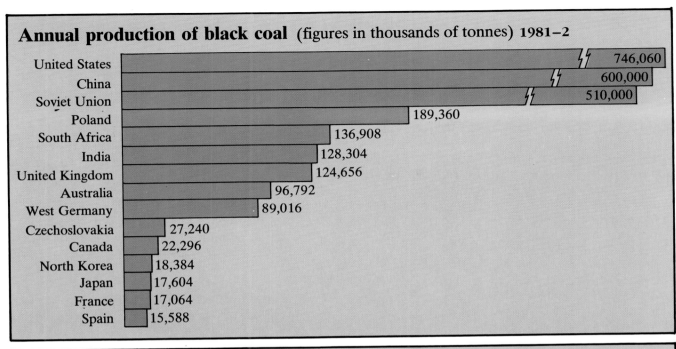

Annual production of black coal (figures in thousands of tonnes) 1981–2

Country	Production
United States	746,060
China	600,000
Soviet Union	510,000
Poland	189,360
South Africa	136,908
India	128,304
United Kingdom	124,656
Australia	96,792
West Germany	89,016
Czechoslovakia	27,240
Canada	22,296
North Korea	18,384
Japan	17,604
France	17,064
Spain	15,588

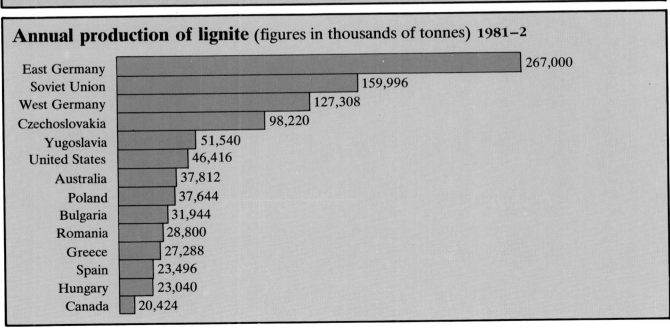

Annual production of lignite (figures in thousands of tonnes) 1981–2

Country	Production
East Germany	267,000
Soviet Union	159,996
West Germany	127,308
Czechoslovakia	98,220
Yugoslavia	51,540
United States	46,416
Australia	37,812
Poland	37,644
Bulgaria	31,944
Romania	28,800
Greece	27,288
Spain	23,496
Hungary	23,040
Canada	20,424

Glossary

Adit A tunnel driven into a hillside to reach an underground coal seam.

Anthracite A very hard form of coal.

Bituminous A description given to many substances that contain carbon and hydrogen.

Bunker A large container for storing coal.

Coal measures The layers of rock in the ground that contain coal seams.

Colliery British name for a coal mine.

Density The weight of a substance in relation to its size. Something of high density, such as lead, takes up less space than the same weight of a low density material such as aluminium.

Face The exposed surface from which coal is cut.

Fault A break in the Earth's crust which results in the rocks either side not matching.

Firedamp Methane gas, which burns and explodes very easily.

Fossil The remains of prehistoric animals or plants preserved as stone.

Geologist A person who studies the structure of the Earth.

Laser A device that emits a narrow beam of concentrated light.

Lignite A low quality coal, often called brown coal because of its colour.

Mudstone A sedimentary rock formed from mud.

Opencast mining Mining coal near the surface by removing the soil and rock above it. The Australian term is open cut, and the American term is strip mining.

Outcrop Part of a layer of rock or a coal seam that appears above ground level.

Radioactivity The emission of radiation from atomic nuclei.

Rank The grade of a coal, according to how much carbon it contains. Peat is the lowest rank, anthracite the highest.

Road A main tunnel in a mine.

Seam A layer or bed of coal.

Sedimentary rock Rock formed by the accumulation of organic material deposited by water, ice or wind.

Seismic Relating to earthquakes, or artificially-produced shocks in the ground.

Sensor An electronic device that detects and responds to a signal such as heat or smoke.

Shale A fine-grained sedimentary rock formed from clay.

Smelting Heating metal-bearing rock to extract the metal.

Specific gravity The relationship of the density of an object to that of water.

Strata Layers of rock.

Subsidence The gradual sinking of the ground.

Volatile A substance that turns readily from liquid to gas, usually highly inflammable.

Sources of further information

For more information about coalmining in Britain contact:
The Press Office, British Coal, Hobart House, Grosvenor Place, London, SW1X 7AE
In the USA contact:
The National Coal Association, 1130 17th Street NW, Washington DC 20036, USA
In Australia contact:
The Bureau of Mineral Resources, Canberra, ACT

Books to read

Coal, its Origin and Occurrence (National Coal Board, 1979)
COX, S. *Mineworker* (Kestrel, 1971)
DAVEY, J. *Mining Coal* (A. & C. Black, 1976)
PHILIPPE, J. *Coal* (Chambers, 1976)
WHITE, C. J. *An Introduction to the Coalmining Industry* (Colin Venton, 1971)

Picture acknowledgements

The author and publishers would like to thank the following for allowing illustrations to be reproduced in this book: British Coal frontispiece, 7, 16, 17, 19 (top), 20, 21, 23, 24, 25, 26, 27, 28, 29, 30, 32, 33, 34, 35, 36 (top), 38, 39, 40, 41; Bruce Coleman 9; Chris Fairclough 6, 12; GeoScience Features 11; Popperfoto 37; Solid Fuel Advisory Service 13; John Topham Picture Library 36 (left); vdn Picture Library 31; Malcolm S. Walker 8, 10, 15, 22, 42, 43, 44–5; all other pictures from the Wayland Picture Library.

Index